Caring for Your
Baby

an easy-to-follow guide

Caring for Your
Baby

an easy-to-follow guide

Naia Edwards

Contents

Introduction

Caring for your new baby is perhaps the most important job you will ever do and certainly the one that requires the most dedication and responsibility. From the moment you become a parent, you take on a full-time job; you must be available for your baby whenever she needs you, day or night. This responsibility may seem overwhelming at first and you may worry about how you'll manage, especially if you haven't had much experience with babies before. But although being a parent may be hard work, it becomes easier as you become more practised. Your baby's needs are only basic human needs: to be fed and kept clean, warm and safe. And perhaps most importantly of all, your baby needs to be loved. While her requirements will change as she gets older, these basic needs will stay the same. Caring for your baby is the most rewarding job you will ever do. Enjoy it!

Please note that to avoid confusion the baby has always been referred to as 'she' but this could just as easily have been 'he'.

Chapter 1

HANDLING YOUR BABY How to hold, handle and carry your baby

Holding, handling and carrying your baby are practical necessities while she is unable to support herself, but just as importantly they are emotional necessities, too. Your touch and embrace will make her feel warm, secure and loved.

To begin with you may feel quite tentative about holding your baby but it won't be long before your confidence grows and it will seem like the easiest thing in the world. As your baby grows older and stronger the way you hold her will change, but the comfort it provides will always stay the same.

Holding your newborn baby

Moments after your baby is born, she will be put in your arms to hold. No one needs to tell you what to do; it will be instinctive to hold her close to you, touch her, stroke her and look at her in wonder and amazement! You may lie together in the delivery room, holding her for quite some time as you start to get to know each other; this skin-to-skin contact will be soothing and calming for both of you. Recent research indicates that having lengthy close physical contact with your baby in the first hour after birth strengthens the bonding process and improves your mothering skills, helping you become more confident and intuitive.

Handling your newborn baby: looking at your newborn baby and marvelling at how tiny and vulnerable she is may make you worry about holding her and hurting her. Don't be nervous. It will come naturally to you to be gentle with your baby and to avoid making sudden noises or movements that may startle her. Remember, newborn babies are much stronger than they look.

Supporting the head: until your baby is about four weeks old she will have very little control of her head. You may have noticed how big her head is in comparison with the rest of her body – it makes up 25 per cent of her total body weight. As her neck muscles are very weak you need to help support her head whenever you are holding, lifting or carrying her around. She will need her head supported for the first three months.

Picking up your baby: your newborn baby will spend most of her time lying flat on her back when you are not holding her. Tiny babies don't wriggle or move very much, so they're easier to pick up. When you pick your baby up from lying down, make sure that all your movements are gentle and smooth.

Back support method: this is probably the method you should try first and is the easiest way to pick up your baby when she is lying down. This is also the method that gives your baby the most support so it is particularly good for very young babies.

1. Slide one hand underneath your baby's head with the base of your hand supporting her neck and your fingers cupping her head.

2. Slide your other hand underneath her bottom and lower back.

3. Gently, but confidently, lift her towards you to hold her in one of the different carrying methods (see pages 9– 10).

Under the arm method: this is particularly useful when picking up your baby from a car seat or other sitting position, although you can use it to pick up a baby who is lying down, too. It is the easiest way to pick up an older baby.

1. Put your hands underneath your baby's arms, with your thumbs on her chest and your fingers stretched up to support the back of her head.

2. Lift her up gently and bring her towards you to hold her in a carrying position.

Carrying your baby: there are many different ways to carry your baby and you will need to experiment to find the most comfortable position for you and the most enjoyable for your baby. Sometimes she will want to be comforted and held close to you; sometimes she will want to face out and look at the world around her; other times she will want to be rocked. Here are some different positions you can try:

Cradle carry position: this is a nice position for looking at your baby. Place her head in the crook of your arm, while your hand supports her under her bottom. Her spine will rest against your forearm. Use your other arm to give additional support across her body, cradling her head in your hand. As you become more confident at handling your baby, you will be able to hold her in this position with just one hand.

Upright position: this is a good way to carry your baby when she's asleep. Hold her with her head to one side against your shoulder and her body close to you. Use one arm to support her underneath her bottom and the other arm to hold her head and back. The slight pressure on her tummy may help if she is windy.

Over the shoulder position: this is similar to the upright position and is equally good for relieving windy tummies. However, instead of holding her head against your shoulder, raise her up a little so that her tummy is against your shoulder and her head and neck are resting over it. Support her bottom with one hand and her head with the other.

Tummy position: this position seems to comfort a lot of babies. Again, it can help bring up wind and can also be used to help relieve colic *(see pages 53–54)*. Hold your baby so that she is lying with her tummy along your forearm, and her head in the crook of your arm. Her head should face away from you. Place your other arm between her legs to hold her securely.

Outward-facing position: your baby will like this position, particularly when she is feeling sociable or bored. Hold her so that she faces outwards and can see what's going on around her. Make a seat under her bottom with one hand and put your other arm across her chest.

TOP TIP
As your baby gets heavier, remember to bend your knees rather than your torso when you lift her to avoid straining your back.

Handling and carrying from 3–12 months

Once your baby's neck muscles are stronger, from around three months old, you do not need to worry so much about supporting her head. This makes it easier to hold her with one hand and means you don't have to be so gentle. Sometimes your baby may enjoy being picked up and whizzed through the air or swung around before being held close and put into a carrying position. But remember, you will need to hold your baby more firmly as she grows and becomes stronger.

Hip position: now you can carry your baby on your hip with her legs straddled either side of you. Use one hand to hold her bottom and the other hand to help support her back, if necessary. This back support is important if your baby has a tendency to make sudden jerky movements, to stop her from falling backwards.

Baby carriers

Some babies are really only happy when they are being carried or held, and will cry if you start to put them down. There is nothing wrong with this and you won't be spoiling your baby if you do pick her up and hold her, but holding your baby in your arms for long periods of time is not always practical.

Slings: using a baby sling is an ideal way to hold and carry your baby as it allows you to keep her close to you without using your arms. Made out of fabric, baby slings are strapped around your body with supports for your baby's head and spine. Your baby fits in snugly and you can walk everywhere with her like this, leaving your hands free to do other things. There is a huge range available.

Make sure you buy one that can be used from the moment your baby is born right through to when she is a toddler. Your older baby will enjoy being carried in it facing out so that she can see what's going on around her.

Baby car seats: if you gave birth to your baby in hospital and arrived by car, you won't be allowed to leave with your baby unless you have a baby car seat – it is illegal to travel without one. Here are a few things to bear in mind when choosing your car seat:

TOP TIP
Even if you drive a lot of the time, you will find it is beneficial to you and your baby to go for regular walks.

- Make sure that your car seat has a headhugger to support your baby's head and neck while she is under three months.

- If your car has front-seat airbags, you must strap the car seat into the back of the car.

- Check how long the car seat will be suitable for your baby. This depends on her weight and not her age. If your baby is too heavy for the weight specified she may not be adequately protected in the event of an accident.

- Not all car seats fit every car so check that the seat you buy will fit yours; retailers should you allow you to try it out.

Prams and pushchairs

When buying a pram or pushchair think about how and where you will want to use it. Babies under 12 weeks old need to be able to lie flat; older babies will want to sit up and look around.

Traditional prams: these are large and spacious, giving your baby plenty of room to lie flat. As she gets bigger, you can prop the mattress up so that she can see more. There is also room for her to sit up unsupported once she is able to. The drawback is that prams take up a lot of space, tend to be heavy and are not easily portable – so not convenient for putting in the car. They are also expensive.

Three-in-one/two-in-one pram/pushchairs: these are modern-style prams that convert into pushchairs so that they can be used from the birth of your baby until she is much older. Some are designed so that you can alter the direction of the seat, so your baby can either face you or face outwards. The drawback is that they tend to be quite heavy.

All-terrain pushchairs: these pushchairs have three wheels: one at the front and two at the back. They are very light and manoeuvrable and easy to push on any terrain. Most have a facility for your baby to lie flat, which then converts to an upright position.

Travel systems: these are designed to combine a car seat, pushchair and pram all in one, making them very versatile.

Strollers or buggies: these are lightweight pushchairs that fold up very easily and are suitable for a toddler who doesn't need to spend all her time in the pushchair. Most strollers have seats that can be unclipped to a reclining position.

SAFETY FIRST

Whatever type of pram or pushchair you decide to buy, it is important to remember some basic rules of safety during use.

- **Always apply the brakes when you stop, even if you're on a flat surface.**

- **Never leave your baby/child unattended.**

- **Check the safety locks on your pushchair to make sure that it doesn't accidentally fold up during use.**

- **Use a safety harness.**

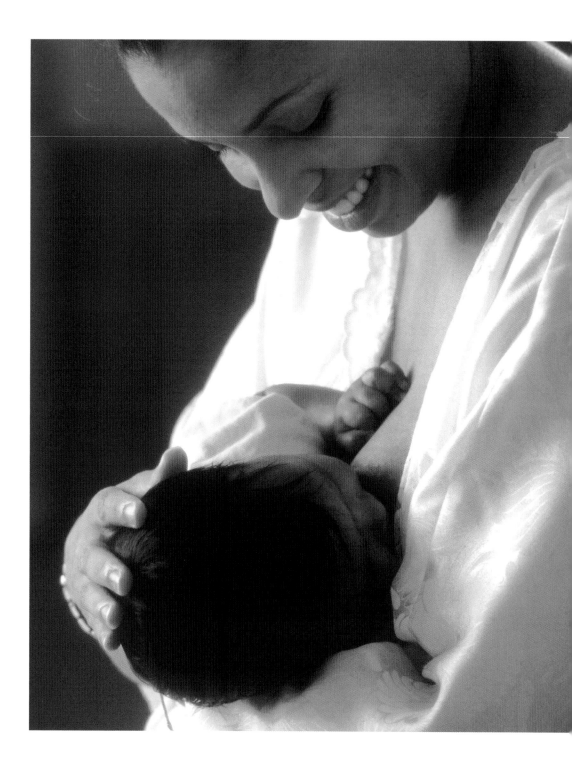

Chapter 2

FEEDING YOUR BABY
What you need, and what to do

One of the first things you will do for your baby once she is born is feed her. Feeding is not only essential for her physical survival – providing her with the nutrients she needs to help her to grow and develop healthily – it is also an opportunity to establish a close emotional bond between the two of you.

How you feed your baby will change over the course of the first year. To begin with there are only two ways of feeding your baby: breastfeeding or bottle-feeding formula milk.

Breastfeeding

As with all aspects of caring for your baby, you should do what works best for you but bear in mind that breast milk is recommended by the World Health Organization as the best food for your baby for the first six months of her life. This is because it contains antibodies that help to protect her from illness and disease; it is also uniquely tailored to provide her with the specific balance of minerals, fats, protein and vitamins that she needs. The minerals and vitamins are easily absorbed because breast milk is easy for your baby to digest.

You will benefit from breastfeeding, too. It is good for your health, helping to protect you from breast cancer and other cancers; it is good for your figure because breastfeeding releases hormones to help your uterus contract and get back to its normal size quickly, as well as using up a lot of calories; and it's good for your finances because breast milk is free. You also won't need to worry about buying tins of formula milk, bottles and sterilising equipment.

Before you start: what you'll need

Here are a few items that will make it easier and more comfortable to breastfeed:

Nursing bras: you will need several of these. They have special cup openings so that you can reveal your breast without having to undo the whole bra.

Breast pads: these fit inside your nursing bras to absorb excess milk leaking and prevent damp patches staining your clothes.

Muslin cloths: these are very useful for all sorts of mopping up, but especially for cleaning up baby sick. An absorbent muslin cloth worn over your shoulder, under your baby's chin, will protect your clothes.

Breastfeeding in the first few days

As soon as possible after your baby is born, hold her close to your breast to see if she 'roots' for it – that is, opens her mouth looking for your breast. She probably won't suck for long, but it should be enough to give you an idea of what it feels like. The sucking action will send messages to your brain to release hormones that stimulate the muscles of the breast to squeeze out milk. This is called the let down reflex. You may feel a slight tingling or pain in your nipple when let down occurs, or you might not feel anything at all.

The milk you produce in the first 72 hours is called colostrum. This is thicker and richer than the milk you produce later and is yellow in colour. It is full of energy-providing nutrients, and antibodies to strengthen your baby's immune system.

After four or five days your mature milk will come through. This consists of a thirst-quenching, watery foremilk (which your baby gets when she first starts to suck), followed by the thicker hindmilk, which is rich in nutrients and satisfies your baby's hunger.

How to breastfeed

Although breastfeeding is the natural way to feed your baby, you will need to learn how to do it. It may take a bit of patience and practise.

Your midwife, health visitor or breastfeeding supporter will be able to give you help and support. Even if everything seems to be going well, it's worth asking a health professional to check that you are doing it properly, for your own reassurance as well as to avoid any problems later on. Here are some basic steps:

Find the right positions for you and your baby: there are lots of different ways to hold your baby while you feed her and you will need to experiment to see what feels most comfortable for you. But whether you choose to sit up or lie down when you feed it's important to remember the following:

● Your baby should always be lying on her side, not on her back.

● Her nose needs to be at the same height as your nipple.

● Her back should be in a straight line, so that she doesn't have to turn her head to feed.

● She should be tucked in as close to you as possible.

Get your baby to open her mouth as wide as possible: she needs to get both your nipple and the dark area around your nipple (called the areola), into her mouth. You can encourage her to open her mouth by stroking her cheek or upper lip with your nipple.

Bring your baby to your breast and get her to latch on: getting your baby properly attached to your breast is the key to successful breastfeeding. Her head should be tilted back slightly so that her nose is level with your nipple, but clear of your breast so that she can breathe easily. Aim your nipple over your baby's tongue and towards the roof of her mouth. If it feels painful, slide your finger into your baby's mouth to break the latch and try again.

Make sure your baby is sucking properly: after the first few hungry gulps, your baby will settle down to a more regular rhythm of feeding. You should be able to hear her suck, suck, suck, swallow and then repeat the pattern. Make sure she empties your breast before offering her the other one if she's still hungry.

TOP TIP
Breastfeeding can make you feel very thirsty. Make sure you have a glass of water by your side before you start to feed.

Burp her then change her nappy: sit your baby on your lap or hold her over your shoulder *(see page 10)* and rub her back gently to bring up any wind she might have swallowed while you were feeding her. You might need to do this once or several times during the feed, or just at the end of a feed.

How to check your baby is getting enough milk

There are two main indicators that your baby is getting enough milk:

Weight gain: during the first week or so your baby may lose up to 10 per cent of her birth weight; after that she should steadily gain weight if she is feeding well.

Wet nappies: checking your baby's nappies is another good way to judge whether she is getting enough milk. After the first few days she should be wetting around 6–8 nappies a day.

Expressing breast milk

After you have established breastfeeding (usually after about six weeks), you may find that expressing your milk helps you to keep on going. It is a method that involves squeezing milk out of your breasts, either manually or with a pump, so that it can be stored in bottles and given to your baby later. This also allows someone else to feed your baby with your milk, and can be particularly useful if you are going back to work or if you simply want to go out for an evening without your baby.

Expressing by hand: this takes time and patience, but will get easier with practise. It's usually easier to do it in the morning when you have a full milk supply.

1. Make sure your hands are clean before you start.

2. Sit at a table with a sterilised bowl or container under your breast.

3. Hold your breast in a C-hold, placing your thumb at the top edge of the areola (the dark skin around your nipple) and use the rest of your hand to cup your breast underneath.

4. Carefully squeeze your finger and thumb together and pull forward.

5. Continue doing this in a rhythmic way until the milk flows.

Using a pump: if you are planning to express on a regular basis, electric or manual breast pumps, which come with full instructions, are often faster and more efficient. It is possible to hire pumps from the hospital or organisations such as the National Childbirth Trust *(see page 70).*

GETTING SUPPORT
Breastfeeding isn't always easy, so you may find it difficult to begin with. Any problems can usually be overcome with help and support. If you are worried or have any concerns, check with your midwife, health visitor or breastfeeding supporter.

Bottle-feeding

Whether you have decided to bottle-feed your baby from birth or whether you are switching to bottle-feeding from breastfeeding, you can be sure that your baby will be getting all the essential nutrients she needs to grow and develop healthily. Although formula milk is not an exact reproduction of breast milk and does not contain protective antibodies, some mothers feel reassured that they can tell how much milk their baby has drunk during bottle-feeding and prefer being able to share feeding with a partner.

WHAT YOU WILL NEED
- Formula milk
- Bottles – at least six
- Teats – as many as you have bottles; try slow-flowing teats to begin with
- Bottle and teat brushes
- Kettle
- Steriliser

Cleaning and sterilising your equipment

Because small babies are particularly vulnerable to infections, all the equipment you use to feed your baby must be carefully washed and then sterilised to kill off any bacteria.

There are several ways to sterilise equipment, including using cold water and sterilising tablets or solution. The quickest, though not the cheapest, way to sterilise things is in specially made steamers. Electric and microwave versions are available which produce enough steam to sterilise equipment in a matter of minutes.

How to prepare a feed

1. Clean the surface where you will be preparing the feeds and wash your hands.

2. Boil fresh tap water in a kettle or pan. Water that has been boiled repeatedly in a kettle should not be used because it will contain too much sodium.

3. Leave the boiled water to cool, but not for more than half an hour. Official guidelines say that the water should not be less than 70°C (158°F) when you add the formula.

4. Pour the required amount of water into the sterilised bottles and then add the precise amount of formula, following the directions on the tin. The number of scoops of powder depends on the weight/age of your baby. It's very important to add the powder to the water and not the other way round so that you ensure you get the right quantity. If you add too much or too little powder, your baby could become ill. Always use a sterilised knife to level off each scoop.

5. Fit the teat and cap back onto the bottle then shake to mix up the contents.

6. Cool the bottle by holding it in a jug of cold water or under a running tap. It should be lukewarm, just above body temperature. Test it by shaking a few drops onto the inside of your wrist.

7. Once your baby has drunk from a bottle, throw away any remaining milk that has not been used within two hours.

STORING BOTTLED MILK

In the past, it was common to make up all the bottles your baby needed for the day in one go. However, in November 2005 the Department of Health changed its advice and now recommends that a fresh bottle is made up for each feed. This is because formula milk is not sterile and there is a small risk of contamination from microorganisms if made up formula is kept. If you need to prepare bottles in advance, the advice is to store freshly boiled water in bottles which you can warm up when you need it and then add the formula milk at the last minute.

How to bottle-feed your baby

1. Find a comfortable and quiet place to feed your baby.

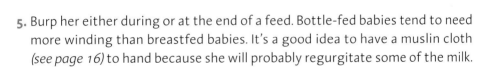

2. Hold your baby with her head in the crook of your arm and bring her in close to you *(see page 9)*. Her head should be higher than her stomach to help digestion, and her back should be straight, not rounded, to prevent her from swallowing too much air.

3. Tip the bottle up so that the teat fills with milk and not air and keep it tilted all the time you are feeding her.

4. Use the time while your baby is feeding to bond with her. Smile, sing, or talk softly to her. Let her take as much time as she likes to feed.

5. Burp her either during or at the end of a feed. Bottle-fed babies tend to need more winding than breastfed babies. It's a good idea to have a muslin cloth *(see page 16)* to hand because she will probably regurgitate some of the milk.

How much and how often to feed your baby

The advice for how much to feed your newborn baby is the same as for breastfed babies: be led by your baby, feed her as often as she asks for it and don't worry how often she wants feeding. In the early days she will need to be fed little and often, possibly only 50ml (1½fl oz) every one or two hours.

By the time she is two or three weeks old, your baby may be able to go for longer between feeds and she will probably be taking around 85ml (3fl oz) every 2½–3 hours.

A feeding pattern will probably emerge quite soon. If your baby is feeding roughly every three hours, she will be taking 6–8 feeds a day. The amount she drinks will steadily increase from 85–113ml (3–4 fl oz) at one month to as much as

TOP TIP
Never prop up a bottle and leave your baby to feed herself as she could choke.

TOP TIP

Freeze puréed vegetables and fruit in ice-cube trays. When you want to feed your baby, simply pop out one or two frozen cubes of food and heat them in a pan or tip them into clearly-labelled freezer bags – make a note of the date and the contents) – for storage in the freezer.

198–227ml (7-8fl oz) by the time she is four months old when she will probably have settled into a pattern of five feeds a day.

Night feeds: to begin with your baby will need feeding at night probably between 10–11pm and then again between 2–3am. But as early as two months old, or 5kg (11lb) in weight, she may have dropped the feed in the early hours of the morning so that you and your baby can enjoy a period of 7–8 hours' uninterrupted sleep.

INTRODUCING SOLIDS

Until your baby is six months old, current Department of Health guidelines recommend that breast milk or formula milk is all she needs. But by the time she reaches six months, she will almost definitely be ready to try some solid food. To begin with, solid food should only be given in addition to your baby's milk feeds. The weaning process from milk to solids is a gradual one, not to mention messy and fun!

WHAT YOU NEED

- Highchair – for when your baby can sit unsupported.
- Bibs – lots of them! The soft wipe-clean ones are great.
- Baby spoons with rubber tips.
- Plastic baby bowls with suction cups underneath to prevent them from moving.

The first time you feed your baby

1. Prepare a small amount of food in a baby bowl. The Department of Health recommends iron-enriched infant rice cereal as a starter food, mixed with breast or formula milk to form a runny consistency.

2. Give your baby about half of her normal milk feed and then, while she is sitting on your lap – still hungry, but not desperate – offer her some of the cereal on the end of your finger or on the tip of a plastic baby teaspoon.

3. Watch her expression as she has her first taste of something new! She may screw up her face and immediately spit it out, or she may look surprised but decide she likes it and open her mouth for more. One taste may be enough for her first time before you give her the rest of her milk feed.

At first your baby will eat very little solid food and it is important not to rush her. She will gradually take more, and by the end of the first week she may be eating 3–4 teaspoons of baby cereal a day.

You can then start to introduce other new foods and make them slightly less runny. Try one food at a time to check for allergic reactions and to work out her preferences. If your baby doesn't finish all the food in her bowl, discard it, rather than saving it for later, to avoid bacteria forming and making your baby ill. It's also important to remember that defrosted food can only be warmed up once.

TOP TIP
Introduce new foods at lunchtime or earlier in the day so that if the food disagrees with your baby the effects will become apparent before bedtime and you will avoid a disturbed night.

Giving your baby drinks

Once your baby is eating solids she will get thirsty, too. The best drink to give her in addition to her milk is cooled boiled water, which she should drink out of a beaker with a soft spout. It's best to avoid giving fruit juices and squashes because the sugar may damage her new teeth.

FEEDING GUIDELINES

6–7 months: just starting solids

- Breakfast – breast or formula milk.
- Mid-morning – breast or formula milk.
- Lunch – 1–3 teaspoons of baby rice or baby cereal mixed with breast or formula milk.
- Mid-afternoon – breast or formula milk.
- Supper – breast or formula milk.
- Bedtime – breast or formula milk.

Two weeks after starting solids

You can add puréed fruit or vegetables to the lunchtime cereal or baby rice. It's a good idea to try giving your baby vegetables before giving her fruit so that she doesn't develop too much of a 'sweet tooth' and turn her nose up at less sweet-tasting vegetables.

7–8 months: 4–6 weeks after starting solids

Give solids at lunchtime and teatime, gradually increasing the amount. Your baby should still be having four milk feeds a day. Try introducing foods she can hold and feed herself with like cooked carrot sticks or breadsticks. This helps improve hand–eye coordination, too, but be prepared for some mess! You can increase the thickness of the foods you give her; include some soft lumps and mashed foods. Start giving her more starchy foods such as bread and pasta.

8–12 months

Your baby will now be eating three meals a day plus fruit or yoghurt for pudding at lunch- and teatime too! She will also still be having three separate milk feeds.

From 12 months

By the time your baby is a year old, she will be able to eat most foods and can have full-fat cows' milk to drink. Before she's a year old you can use cows' milk to mix her food, but it doesn't contain enough iron or minerals to form the basis of her milk feed on its own.

FIRST FOODS TO TRY

- Baby rice or baby cereal with breast or formula milk added.

- Vegetables like carrot, potato, parsnip and butternut squash can be steamed (without adding salt to the water) and then mashed.

- Fruit such as bananas and pears are good because you can just mash them. Hard fruit like apples should be cooked and then puréed.

FOODS TO AVOID
Never feed your baby:

- Salt or salty food. From seven months babies can have a maximum of 1g of salt a day, but still avoid salty food such as sausages, cheese or bacon and processed food that is not made specifically for babies and which can have a high salt content.

- Sugar or sugary food as it's important not to encourage a sweet tooth, which might cause damage and decay to your baby's new teeth.

- Wheat, nuts and seeds. These are among several foods that can cause allergic reactions in babies. It's best to avoid offering your baby these foods before 7 months.

- Citrus fruit or eggs until she is eight months old.

- Honey until she is one year old because of the risk of botulism, a type of food poisoning caused by bacteria.

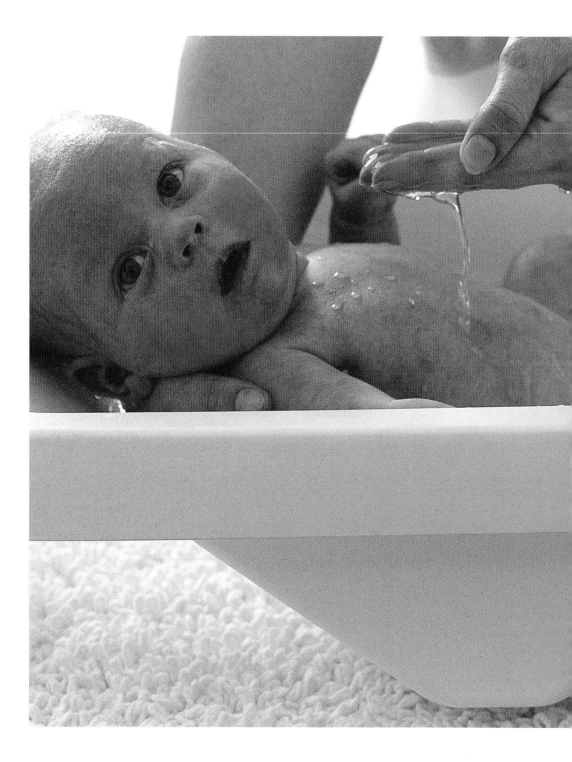

Chapter 3

EVERYDAY CARE
Bathing, nappy changing and dressing

Bathing or washing your baby and changing her nappy to keep her clean will soon become routine. In the first few months, your baby does not need to be bathed every day, but you will need to clean her nappy area, the creases and folds in her skin, frequently. However, once you have got used to holding your baby in the bath, you may decide to make bathtime part of your daily routine because it can be so relaxing and enjoyable for both you and your baby.

Your baby will get much dirtier when she is old enough to crawl around, so you will probably find that a daily bath before bedtime is the easiest way to clean her. By this time your baby will look forward to her bath as a fun place to play.

Washing your newborn baby

Your newborn baby will only need a bath a couple of times a week. She certainly won't need a full bath straight away, but certain areas of her body will need to be washed.

One way to wash her is to 'top and tail' her – that is, to wash her face and bottom, which are the areas that need it most – until you feel confident that you are holding your baby securely. First wash her face using cotton wool that has been dipped in warm water and then squeezed fairly dry. Using a new piece of cotton wool for each part of her face, wipe her eyes from the nose outwards, then her nose and then clean around her ears (but not inside them). Then make sure her genitals and bottom are clean *(see page 35)*.

Cleaning the umbilical cord: for the first 10 days or so after your baby is born, a part of the umbilical cord which connected you to your baby in the womb will still be attached to her tummy button. Gently clean around it with cotton wool and warm water every day, but otherwise leave it alone. The stump should fall off and be healed after 10– 14 days. If you notice any yellow discharge or if it smells nasty, seek advice from your midwife or health visitor.

Sponge bath: this is a sort of midway point between topping and tailing *(see above)* and a full-blown bath. It's particularly good if your baby doesn't like being undressed and exposed, because you remove her clothes in stages, as you wash her; she is never completely naked. You can sit her on your lap or lie her down on a changing mat, depending on which you find easiest, and then gently wash each part of her body in turn. Pay special attention to the creases and folds in her skin and the area under the neck which collects spilled milk. Dry her with a towel and put her clothes back on before moving onto washing the next part of her body. Talcum powder is no longer recommended because it can dry out your baby's natural skin oils and is not good for her lungs if inhaled.

Hair washing: your baby should really have her hair (or head, if she doesn't have much hair) washed several times a week to prevent scaly skin forming on the scalp – a common condition known as cradle cap. This can be done quite separately from bathtime if you prefer.

1. Fill a bowl or baby bath with warm water and wrap your baby securely in a towel.

2. Hold her under your arm in a 'rugby hold' so that she is lying at your side with her upper body supported by your forearm and her toes pointing behind you. Her head should be tilted back in your hand over the bowl or bath.

3. With your free hand use a sponge or flannel to squeeze water carefully over her head, making sure that no water gets in her eyes.

4. Use a small amount of non-sting baby shampoo and rub it in gently, using the flat of your hand, before rinsing it off again. You can wash the diamond-shaped soft spot in the middle of your baby's head, called the fontanelle, too – don't worry, you won't hurt her.

5. Dry her hair with a towel and then use a baby comb or soft baby brush. This will help prevent cradle cap.

TRIMMING YOUR BABY'S NAILS

Newborn babies can have quite long, sharp fingernails. Scratch mittens will stop your baby from scratching her face when she's tiny. After the first few weeks, you can trim your baby's nails with baby scissors. Toenails grow more slowly than fingernails so will only need trimming every month or so with baby scissors.

Giving your baby a bath: use a baby bath or washing-up bowl. You can bath your baby in any room as long as it is warm enough.

1. If you are using a specially designed baby bath it may come with a stand so that you can bath her at hip height. Otherwise put your bath or washing-up bowl on a work top at a comfortable height for you to lean over and bath her.

TOP TIP
Having a bath with your baby can be a lovely experience. You and you will both enjoy the intimacy of the skin-to-skin contact.

2. Fill the bath with about 5–8cms (2–3in) of warm water. Use your elbow, not your

hand, to test the temperature, which should feel warm but not too hot. If you have a thermometer, the ideal temperature is 37– 37.5°C (98– 99.5°F).

3. Make sure you have everything you need for your baby's bath before you undress her: sponge or flannel, cotton wool to clean her eyes, shampoo if you are going to wash her hair in the bath, towel laid out on the changing mat, and a nappy and clean clothes for after her bath. You shouldn't use any soap or bubble bath to begin with as this can dry out your baby's skin.

4. When you are ready to put her in the bath, gently but firmly hold her with her head in the crook of your arm and your hand under her armpit, while your other hand supports her bottom. As you lower her into the water, reassure her with a smile and talk to her softly.

5. The bottom of the bath will support your baby's bottom and back so you only need to use one hand to support her head and neck by holding her under her arm. Use your free hand to wash her with the sponge or flannel.

6. Wash your baby gently all over her body, paying particular attention to her creases and under her neck. Use damp cotton wool to wash her face *(see page 30)*.

7. When you have finished, use both hands to lift your baby from the bath. Wrap her in the towel you laid out ready for her on her changing mat then pat her dry, put her nappy on and dress her again.

Moving to the big bath: by the time your baby is three or four months old, she will have grown too big for the baby bath, and you will feel much more confident holding her and transferring her to the normal bath. Bathtime will start to become more of a playtime, too. You can give her bath toys to play with and she can enjoy having bubbles in the water. You might want to put an anti-slip mat in the bottom of the bath to stop her from slipping over. Remember that you must *never* leave a baby of any age alone in a bath, even for a short time.

TOP TIP
Tuck a towel into the front of your clothes so that when you lift your baby out of the bath you can wrap her up in the towel while holding her close to you giving her warmth and security at the same time as keeping you dry!

Changing your baby's nappy

In the early months, your baby may wet her nappy up to eight times a day and, if she has sensitive skin, need you to change it each time – so even if you find changing a nappy a little awkward at first, in a relatively short space of time you will become very practised at it! If your baby's skin is not too sensitive, you won't necessarily need to change her nappy every time she wets it. But you should change it before or after every feed, and every time she has a soiled nappy, to prevent sore nappy rash and a nasty smell.

Nappy rash: however frequently you change your baby's nappy, she is likely to get nappy rash at some point. If an area of skin around the bottom appears to be red, inflamed and sore-looking, with little spots or blisters, your baby has nappy rash. It can be caused by a number of things, including moisture, urine and, if your baby has sensitive skin, chemicals used in baby wipes or nappies.

What to do: make sure your baby's nappy is changed as frequently as you can and that she is kept clean and dry. If possible, try to give your baby some bare-bottom time every day so that she gets air to the sore bit – this should help the area to dry more quickly heal. Various healing nappy creams are also available. Nappy rash normally disappears within a few days. If it gets worse or becomes infected, seek advice from your health visitor or doctor.

Different types of nappy: the first thing you have to do is decide what type of nappy to use – disposable or washable nappies. There are advantages and disadvantages to both.

Disposable nappies: pros

● Very easy to use.

● No dirty washing is required; you simply throw the used nappy away.

● Very absorbent and capable of holding a lot of urine while keeping your baby's bottom dry.

● Convenient for travelling.

Disposable nappies: cons

● Expensive in the long run.

● Wasteful and create a major problem for the environment as they can take a very long time to decompose. Even the newer, biodegradable disposables, which are made without harmful chemicals and decompose more quickly than non-biodegradable nappies, are still harmful to the environment.

Washable nappies: pros

● Cheaper in the long term, after the initial outlay of buying the cloth nappies.

● Kinder to the environment as you are not creating lots of rubbish, though you do need to bear in mind the cost of using the washing machine and washing detergents.

Washable nappies: cons

● Time-consuming as they require a lot of washing. You might want to make use of a nappy laundering service if you have one locally. The cost of this should still be less than the cost of buying disposable nappies.

● Take up more space.

● Depending on the type you buy, they can be more fiddly to put on. Some require nappy pins to secure them, while others have Velcro tabs.

Where to change your baby
Given that you will be doing this a lot, you need to find somewhere at home that

WHAT YOU NEED

- Changing mat
- Nappy – check that you've got the right size according to your baby's weight
- Cotton wool and warm water, or lotion/baby wipes
- Nappy cream
- Nappy bag

is comfortable. Changing your baby on a surface at waist height is often easiest, provided you keep your hand on your baby to stop her from rolling. A purpose-built changing table with safety straps to hold your baby, or any type of work top with a changing mat on top, is ideal and will make it much easier on your back. Alternatively, you can change your baby on a mat on the floor and sit down to change her.

How to change a disposable nappy

1. If your baby has a dirty nappy, try to clean off as much as possible using the front part of the nappy. Lift your baby's legs by holding her ankles together with one hand to remove her dirty nappy from under her bottom with the other hand. Put the dirty nappy in a nappy bag, and tie it up.

2. Use cotton wool and warm water for a young baby or baby wipes for an older baby to clean the rest of your baby's bottom. A girl should be cleaned from her genitals to her bottom to avoid spreading germs. A boy should be wiped clean around the penis and testicles. Don't pull the foreskin back to clean it. Make sure you clean the leg creases, too, as this area can get particularly sore if it isn't cleaned properly.

3. You can apply a nappy cream, which can help to prevent nappy rash, but it isn't essential.

4. Open up the fresh nappy so that it's lying flat with the tabs at the back. Lift your baby's legs up, holding her by her ankles, and slide the back of the nappy underneath her bottom. Bring the front part of the nappy up between her legs and fit it around her tummy. Unpeel the sticky tabs at the back and fasten them over the front of the nappy so that it fits comfortably. You should be able to slide two or three fingers between the nappy and your baby's skin – that's about the right fit.

5. Put your baby somewhere safe, then wash your hands.

Changing your baby's washable nappy

There are three types of washable nappy. The traditional terry nappies are square pieces of cloth that need to be folded and fastened with nappy pins. They have waterproof outer plastic pants and an inner disposable nappy liner which is flushed away. Two-part nappies consist of an inner nappy and separate waterproof outer pants. They are shaped to fit. All-in-one nappies combine the inner part and waterproof outer pants. They are shaped to fit and fasten with velcro tabs.

The instructions below are for folding and putting on a two-part nappy with fasteners.

1. Place the shaped nappy on the changing mat and put a nappy liner on top.

2. Making sure you have all the things you need close at hand, lie your baby flat on the mat and remove her nappy. If she has a dirty nappy you can flush the soiled nappy liner down the loo. Put the cloth nappy in a bucket to soak so that it is easier to wash later.

TOP TIP

Baby boys often tend to wee when you are changing them! To avoid getting wet yourself, place an extra nappy on top of their penis while you change them.

3. Clean your baby's bottom in the same way as described for disposable nappies *(see page 35)*.

4. Lift up your baby's legs and bottom and slide the long top edge of the clean folded nappy underneath. Fold the lower half of the nappy up to your baby's tummy and fasten the poppers or Velcro tabs. Put the outer plastic pants over the top.

5. Put your baby somewhere safe, then wash your hands.

Clothes for your newborn baby

If you don't know what sex your baby is going to be, it's best to opt for neutral colours in a size that will allow some room for growth. Here is a list of basic clothes you will need for the first few months:

- Cotton vests: you will probably need about six of these.

- Sleepsuits: at least eight.

- Cardigans: two or three, depending on the season.

- Socks: four or five pairs.

- Baby tights: one pair in the winter.

- Hats: one.

- Mittens: two pairs.

- Swaddling shawl.

- Snowsuit: one for a winter baby.

WHAT NOT TO WEAR (OR BUY)!

- Clothes that are labelled 'newborn': your baby will grow out of these very quickly unless she is really small. It is much better to buy for 0–3 months.

- Too many clothes: although you will find that you have to change your baby's clothes a surprising number of times in a day – because she's dribbled all over them or sicked up lots of milk, or because her nappy has leaked – you don't want to buy too many clothes. Firstly, you will probably be given a lot of clothes as presents after your baby is born. Secondly, your baby will grow very quickly and if you have too many clothes, the chances are that she may never have time to wear them before she's too big for them.

- Shoes: your baby won't need to wear proper shoes until she can walk. Socks should be enough to keep her feet warm, though the elasticated slipper shoe can be handy for keeping your baby's socks on.

- Clothes made out of synthetic fabrics: it's best to choose cotton clothes as they allow the skin to breathe, and so help to prevent overheating.

- Dry-clean only clothes: your life will be a lot easier if you choose clothes that are machine-washable and can be tumble-dried.

- Fussy and uncomfortable clothes: keep your baby's clothes simple. Elaborate bows and ribbons can be dangerous if your baby gets twisted up in them. Lacy cuffs and collars, while they may look pretty, can irritate your baby and give her rashes.

Dressing your baby

It can take quite a long time to dress your baby and you may feel awkward and clumsy the first few times you do it. Don't worry, your baby will be patient and forgiving. If you do handle her awkwardly, she may display the Moro reflex – an automatic response to sudden movements when she will throw open her arms in startled surprise. She will soon relax and probably be quite passive while you practise taking her clothes on and off her. You will need to be quite practised for your older baby who will be much less patient and more wriggly while you try to dress her! Make sure that where you are dressing your baby is warm. A non-slip changing mat with a towel on the top is a good place to dress her at first. When you are more confident, you may prefer to lay her on your lap with her head on your knees and her feet resting against your tummy.

Putting on a vest:

1. If you are using the wide-necked type of vest, spread open the top of the vest with your thumbs and pull up the rest of the vest with your index fingers. Using your other fingers to gently raise your baby's head, quickly pop the vest over her head, trying not to touch her face (babies don't like things touching their faces) and then put her head down again.

2. Take your baby's arm with one hand and use your other hand to widen the opening of the arm hole of the vest. Guide her arm through the hole and then do the same with her other arm.

3. Pull the rest of the vest down and fasten the poppers between her legs.

Putting on a sleepsuit:

1. Spread out the sleepsuit with the poppers all undone and sides opened out flat.

2. Lay your baby on top of the sleepsuit.

3. Roll up one of the sleeves and put your fingers through the wrist opening to take your baby's hand and guide it through. Then do the same with the other arm.

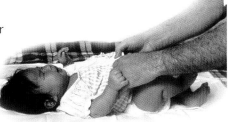

4. To get your baby's legs into the suit, bend one of her knees gently, take her foot and guide it into the foot of the suit. Then do the same with her other leg.

5. Finally, do up all the poppers. It's a good idea to start at the top and gradually work down so that you don't miss any out.

Taking off a sleepsuit

1. Lay your baby on the changing mat and undo all the poppers of her sleepsuit.

2. Use one hand to bend one of her knees and pull her foot out, while your other hand holds onto the foot of the sleepsuit. Then do the same with her other leg.

3. If you just need to change her nappy, lift your baby's legs up by the ankles with one hand while you slide the legs of the sleepsuit to one side.

4. To take off the top part of the sleepsuit, roll up the sleeves of your baby's sleepsuit with one hand while carefully bending her elbow with the other and pulling it out of the sleeve. Then do the same with the other arm.

Taking off a vest

1. Use both hands to pull up the vest around the neck and make as wide an opening as possible.

2. Carefully lift the front of the vest over her head.

3. Lift her head gently to remove the back of the vest.

TOP TIP
From three or four months old when your baby is able to support her head comfortably, you can sit her on your lap to dress and undress her. Make sure you hold her firmly under her arm with one hand while you use your other hand to put on or take off her clothes.

Keeping your baby at the right temperature

A basic rule of thumb is that your newborn baby should be dressed in one more layer of clothing than you are wearing yourself, unless the weather is very hot. If it's more than 24°C (75°F), she will only need one layer of clothing. If you are unsure, feel the back of your baby's neck. If she feels cold, then she will need an extra layer of clothing. Likewise, if she feels hot and sweaty, you will need to remove a layer of clothing.

TOP TIP
If you do up all the zips and poppers on your baby's clothes before putting them into the washing machine it helps them to keep their shape.

Protecting your baby from the sun: if you are going out in the sun you will need to make sure your baby is well protected. A baby's skin is particularly sensitive and can burn very easily, which will be painful and can lead to skin cancer later in life. Sunburn can happen even on a cloudy day. Make sure your baby wears a hat and sun-block cream, which gives maximum protection from UVA and UVB rays.

Washing your baby's clothes

You may be surprised at how much washing you have to do even when your baby is tiny, but especially once you start weaning her onto solid food! It's best to wash your baby's clothes before she wears them for the first time as this will help to ensure they are soft and free from any chemicals that may have been used to make them. Use a washing powder and fabric softener designed for sensitive skin to prevent allergies and irritation. Washable nappies *(see page 34)* should always be washed separately.

Chapter 4

SLEEP Helping your baby to settle and sleep safely

You may hear very different things about babies and sleeping. On the one hand, you will hear how much newborn babies sleep and the phrase 'sleeping like a baby' will ring in your ears. On the other hand you will hear people talking about the sheer exhaustion of looking after a baby owing to the lack of sleep and broken nights. The reason for this is that every baby is different. Some babies will need a lot of sleep and will sleep through the night within weeks. Others may need much less sleep, wake up frequently and take months to sleep through the night. You cannot help what type of baby you are born with, but you can make things easier for you and your baby. And one day, whether it is sooner or later, she will sleep well and you will get a whole night's sleep again.

Where your baby should sleep

Official advice from the Department of Health is that, if possible, your baby should sleep in your bedroom at night for the first six months. Your baby is at her most vulnerable during this time, so having her in your room makes it easier for you to check that she is all right. If you are not able to put your baby in the same room as you, and you are worried, baby monitors that pick up every sound your baby makes, may reassure you.

The next thing to decide is what your baby will sleep in:

A Moses basket: this is a basket with a detachable hood, usually used during the first 2–3 months because it is small and won't overwhelm your baby. It is easily portable so you can move your baby from room to room during the day, but it shouldn't be used to transport your baby outside of the home.

Cot: this can be used from birth or once your baby has outgrown her Moses basket at about three months old. One with drop-down sides makes it much easier for you to lift your baby in and out and you won't risk straining your back. If you are buying a second-hand cot, make sure that you buy a new mattress that fits snugly, so your baby doesn't get herself wedged down the side.

Your bed: if you are breastfeeding, you may find that it is easier to feed your baby at night if she sleeps in bed with you. A recent study of 120 countries showed that 50 per cent of mothers share their bed with their baby, though it doesn't seem to be so popular in the UK and other Western European countries. Some parents are worried about rolling over and accidentally suffocating their baby. In fact, it should be perfectly safe for your baby to share your bed provided that you haven't drunk any alcohol or taken any form of drug (legal or illegal), and that there are no pillows nearby which may suffocate her. It's also not a good idea to sleep with any sibling toddlers. For further advice and information, contact The Foundation for the Study of Infant Deaths *(see page 70).*

Here are some of the pros and cons of sharing your bed with your baby:

Pros

⬤ You don't have to get out of bed to feed her at night.

⬤ You can doze while your baby feeds and settles back to sleep. She may get back to sleep more quickly and easily with the security of having you next to her.

⬤ Some studies claim that babies who sleep in the same bed sleep for longer periods during the night and are more content and sociable in the day.

Cons

⬤ You may worry unnecessarily about rolling on top of your baby and so sleep less well.

⬤ If your baby is used to falling asleep next to you, it may make it more difficult for her to go to sleep at night without you.

⬤ Intimacy in bed between you and your partner will be more difficult.

WHY BABIES NEED SLEEP
Like adults, babies have different cycles of sleep ranging from a light sleep to a dream sleep or REM (Rapid Eye Movement) sleep to a deep sleep and back again. During the dream sleep your baby's brain cells develop and make connections that help her to understand her new world.

How much sleep your baby needs
Tiny babies need a lot more sleep than adults. On average they will sleep around 16 hours a day, though not all at night and with lots of wakeful periods in-between. To begin with, your baby will not be able to distinguish between night-time and daytime and she will need to wake up regularly to be fed. A baby will normally have eight sleeps in a 24-hour period; they can last anything from a few minutes to 2–4 hours. If you are lucky, you may have a baby who sleeps

longer sleeps at night from very early on. If you are not so lucky, you may have a baby who finds night-time her most wakeful time. From around six weeks, your baby's body clock should have adjusted to a pattern of sleeping longer at night. Here's a rough guide to how much your baby might sleep:

- Newborn: 16 hours a day, for 2–4 hours at a time.

- 3 months: 15 hours a day, with a 7–8-hour stretch at night.

- 6 months: 14 hours a day, with an 10-hour stretch at night.

How to help your baby sleep

Don't worry if your baby is very wakeful. It won't harm her and, in fact, there is a theory that babies who spend less time sleeping are more aware of the world around them and will develop learning skills more quickly. But while it may be fine for your baby, it isn't so good for you. Being on call 24 hours a day and woken frequently in the night for weeks on end is shattering and you may find it very hard to cope.

There are many different theories and tips about ways to get your baby to sleep. Some will work for you and your baby and some won't, but it's worth trying out a few ideas. Here are some generally accepted suggestions for things you can do from an early age to encourage your baby to go back to sleep quickly after a feed at night:

1. Try not to let your baby sleep for too long between feeds during the day. The amount of time she is awake during the day will affect how much she sleeps at night. Try to give your baby things to interest and stimulate her – talk to her and play with her. However, it's equally important that she gets enough sleep during the day so that she doesn't get over-tired or overstimulated.

2. Try giving your baby a bedtime routine from quite early on. She may wake up shortly after you put her to bed, but it can still be helpful to you to know that your baby has a bedtime, and at some stage she should recognise this pattern and what it means. Begin with a warm bath to soothe her, then put on a clean nappy and her night-time clothes and then spend some time quietly talking to her and winding down. If you hold her close and gently massage her *(see pages 56–57)*; this should help her feel even more relaxed. Feed her in a

darkened, draught-free room (a temperature of 16–20°C (60–68°F) is about right) and make sure she is properly winded *(see page 18)* before putting her down to sleep.

3. Try not to let your baby fall completely asleep before you put her down. It's helpful if she is still a little awake so that she learns how to go to sleep alone.

4. When she wakes in the night, keep the lighting and your voice low, and make the feed as boring as possible. Try not to chat to her too much or stimulate her.

5. Make sure she is properly winded then put her straight back down again.

6. Don't change her nappy unless you need to.

TOP TIP
You may also find it helpful to wake your baby and feed her just before your bedtime so that you get a few hours' sleep at least before she wakes again for another feed.

Going for a walk and rocking her: almost every baby loves to be rocked or pushed in a pram. When your baby was in the womb she was constantly rocked as you walked around with her, so the familiar motion relaxes her and sends her to sleep. You can push her in her pram outside or around the house, walk with her in a baby sling *(see page 11)*, or simply rock her in your arms. Babies often love the motion of being in a car, too, and this almost always guarantees your baby will sleep. However, she may wake up the minute the engine stops!

Swaddling: some small babies like the feeling of being held tight. Wrapping your baby up in a shawl or cellular blanket is called swaddling. It can make her feel secure and snug, and encourage her to sleep. To swaddle your baby, fold a blanket or shawl in half to make a triangle shape with the longest edge at the top. Put your baby in the middle with her toes pointing towards the bottom tip of the triangle. Fold the bottom tip up over your baby's toes, then wrap first one side of the blanket then the other over your baby and tuck it firmly behind her back. Loosen the swaddle once your baby is asleep to prevent her overheating.

Dummies: opinion is divided about the use of dummies. Some people argue that a dummy can be bad for a baby who is breastfeeding because it can confuse her sucking instinct, and some people disapprove on the grounds that it looks horrible to see a baby with a dummy in her mouth. Conversely, other people argue that some babies have a need to suck, not just for food but because it soothes them. A dummy used in the unsettled period from your baby's first second month can help relax and comfort her, and so make her more likely to sleep. Evidence also now shows that settling your baby with a dummy can reduce the risk of cot death *(see below)*. Don't worry if it falls out of her mouth while she is asleep and don't force a baby to take a dummy if she doesn't want to.

Safe sleeping

When a baby dies suddenly, for no apparent reason, it is called Sudden Infant Death Syndrome (SIDS), or cot death. Although it is thankfully very rare, it has received quite a lot of media coverage, because it is so shocking when it does happen and because no one quite knows why it happens. However, although we don't know the causes, The Foundation for the Study of Infant Deaths *(see page 70)* has recommended ways to reduce the risk of it occurring:

- The safest sleep position for your baby is on her back. Although in the 1970s most babies were put to sleep on their tummies, research has shown that SIDS is far less common in babies who sleep on their backs. Once your baby is old enough to roll over onto her tummy, at about six months, it's fine to let her do this as there is far less risk of SIDS occurring in older babies.

- When you tuck your baby into her cot or Moses basket make sure it is in a 'feet to foot' position – when your baby's feet are at the foot of the cot or basket. This will stop her wriggling down under her covers.

- Make sure you tuck your baby in tight, ensuring her covers come no higher than her shoulders. You do not want sheets or blankets slipping up over her head as this can increase the risk of SIDS.

- Smoking during pregnancy and/or exposure of the baby to smoke after she's born can dramatically increase the risk of SIDS. For this reason ask smokers to smoke outside the house.

TOP TIP
If your baby is unwell and has a fever, it is even more important to check she isn't wearing too many clothes or covered by too much bedding.

Overheating can also increase the risk of SIDS because, unlike older children and adults, young babies are unable to regulate their body temperature. Check the temperature of the room in which she sleeps (it should be no higher than 16–20° C (60–68°F)) and make sure that her clothes and bedding don't make her too hot. (You can buy room temperature guides which come in the form of a card to hang on the wall). In summer, if it's warm, your baby may only need a sheet. The majority of SIDS cases occur in the winter, and this may be because they have been overly wrapped up and have therefore overheated. Cot bumpers, duvets and pillows are not recommended for this reason because they can accidentally cover a baby's head and make her too hot.

Tips for coping with tiredness

For your sanity, it's important to find ways to cope with fatigue:

Sleep when your baby sleeps. After all, even if you have a baby who doesn't sleep the average 16 hours a day, she will still probably be sleeping for about 12 hours. It is extremely tempting to use the time that your baby sleeps during the day to do all those things you don't otherwise have time for, or just to spend some time on your own, but if you can sometimes allow yourself to go to sleep when your baby does, you will find it really does help.

If you have a partner, ask him to help occasionally with night feeds. You can do this even if you're breastfeeding by expressing some of your milk *(see page 20)* into a bottle so that your baby can still benefit from your milk.

Eat and exercise well. A healthy balanced diet and exercise really will give you more energy and help you feel less tired.

Remember that this period of sleeplessness won't last for ever. Your baby will learn to sleep through the night so you will soon feel less tired.

Chapter 5

CRYING Why babies cry and how to soothe them

All babies cry, but some babies cry a lot. Before your baby can talk, or even smile, she can cry, and this is the only way your baby can communicate with you; it is normal for her to cry for several hours a day. Her cry is designed to get your attention and it's very effective! For someone so small, it's amazing how much noise she can make. But if she cries often or isn't easily comforted, or you are unsure why she is crying, it can be very upsetting. It will probably take some time to learn what your baby is trying to tell you. She may be crying for different reasons, such as being hungry, tired, lonely or cold. As your baby gets older, you will both find it easier to work out what the problem is and how to solve it. You will become better at understanding what your baby's cries mean and she will become better at communicating with you so that she doesn't just have to rely on crying.

Why your baby cries

Your newborn baby may cry for a variety of reasons and discovering the cause will be a question of trial and error to begin with. Here are some of the most common and basic reasons why newborn babies cry:

Hunger: if your baby is crying, the first thing to do is to check whether she's hungry. Because your newborn baby's tummy is so tiny, she can only drink small amounts of milk at a time. Each feed will last her about a couple of hours and she will cry to let you know when she needs to be fed again. Pick her up and offer her some milk to see if this soothes her. Once you have finished feeding her, make sure you wind her properly *(see page 18)*. If she has swallowed a lot of air while feeding, she will feel uncomfortable and this will be another reason for her to cry. She will feel a lot better after she's burped.

In need of comfort: a lot of babies like to be held and carried and will cry if you put them down. Cuddling and holding your baby will make her feel secure, warm and loved, and is a perfectly natural thing for both you and your baby to want to do. If she does want to be held all the time, try wearing a baby sling *(see page 10)* so she can feel you close to her and have the reassurance of being held, while you have your hands free to get on with other things.

Tiredness: although your baby is capable of going to sleep almost anywhere – in the pram, your arms, the car, or in the cot – there will be times when it is difficult for her to go to sleep or she resists sleep, and then she will cry because she's tired. If, for example, your baby is played with a lot or she has a lot of visitors and is passed around to be held by different people, she may become overstimulated and

suddenly cry because it's all become a bit too much. As a result, she will need some quiet time away from people and activity, and may need help getting to sleep with some gentle rocking and quiet holding. For this reason try to limit the number of visitors in the early days.

Wet or soiled nappy: while some babies don't seem to notice how wet or dirty their nappy is, others will cry and want their nappy changed immediately. The sooner you can change your baby's nappy the better, as this will help prevent nappy rash *(see page 33)*, which can make your baby very sore and lead to more crying. Some babies will cry when you change their nappy because they don't like having their clothes taken off. As you become practised at nappy changing you will get quicker at it so that it becomes less of an ordeal. Older babies don't seem to mind as much about being exposed and having their nappy changed.

Too hot or too cold: your baby needs to be kept at the right temperature to be comfortable. She may cry if she is too hot or too cold. A comfortable room temperature is around 16–20°C (60–68°F). For sleeping, it's recommended that you use a sheet and cot blankets that you can layer to regulate how warm or cool you want it. When you are dressing her, the general rule is that she will need one more layer of clothes than you are wearing, but it's sensible just to check her temperature by feeling the back of her neck.

Unwell: if your baby is ill or in pain her cry will probably be quite different from her normal cry. It may sound more high-pitched than usual or more insistent. Equally, if your baby normally cries a lot but then seems unnaturally quiet, this may also be an indication that she's not well. If you have checked the most obvious causes for crying and ruled them out, there may be something wrong with your baby. If you are at all worried, call your doctor or talk to your midwife or health visitor.

Colic: colic is often defined by the 'rule of three': a baby has colic if she fusses or cries for more than three hours a day, for more than three days a week, for more than three weeks. And give or take a few hours or weeks, millions of babies fit this diagnosis: they experience bouts of unexplained and inconsolable crying. Colic may start from around two weeks, reach its peak at six weeks and then finally stop at three months when your baby suddenly grows out of it and resumes a more bearable crying pattern of around an hour a day. Colicky babies often have a set crying time – usually in the evening when you are feeling most tired! It can be quite distressing, especially if your baby also pulls her legs up to her chest as if in pain.

Possible explanations: researchers have tried taking x-rays and carrying out tests to see whether colicky babies have something wrong with their intestines, which makes digestion uncomfortable, but so far there appears to be no medical reason for it. While no one is sure why colic happens, there are various theories. The first thing to stress is that colic is not a result of bad parenting. It can happen to any baby, although it tends to happen to more sensitive babies. One theory is that sensitive babies cry more because they find the enormous amount of new things they are experiencing bewildering. Another theory suggests that it might have something to do with diet – either yours if you are breastfeeding and have eaten something that disagrees with your baby, or the type of formula she is having if you are bottle-feeding. If you are concerned about her feeding talk to your health visitor or doctor.

How to soothe and comfort your baby
When your baby cries you will want to calm, comfort and soothe her. In times gone by, it was believed that picking up a crying child too often might encourage her to become demanding and spoilt. It was common to leave a baby to cry and to believe that crying was good exercise for a baby's lungs. Research now suggests that if a crying baby is quickly attended to she is less likely to cry the next day and, later on, she is more likely to be sociable and have advanced communication skills, whereas babies who are left to cry tend to become withdrawn and introverted.

Here are a few things you can try to find out what helps soothe your baby:

Swaddling: many small babies like to be wrapped up tight in swaddling blankets *(see page 47)*. It can be very soothing and help your baby feel secure. It also stops thrashing her arms and legs about and your baby startling herself. Remember to loosen the swaddle once your baby is asleep to prevent her overheating.

Rocking and movement: babies love being rocked, whether it is by you, or in a baby rocking chair or swing. It often becomes automatic to start swaying from side to side as you hold your baby, or jiggling her gently up and down – you may not even realise you are doing it. When your arms are tired, put your baby in her pram and walk her about. Take her outside for a change of scenery – even if it doesn't help her, it may make you feel better! Car journeys often seem to help as well; there are many stories of parents who have spent the early hours of the morning driving their babies around to nowhere in particular to get them to stop crying.

MUSIC AND RHYTHM

Singing lullabies is a traditional way to soothe your baby. You don't have to be a great singer, or even to know the words of the lullaby, for your baby to be comforted by the sound of your voice. If you feel too self-conscious to sing, you can try playing her music – some people say that a baby will be comforted by the music you played when you were pregnant. She will recognise this and be reassured by its familiarity. Music with a rhythmic beat, like the sound of your heartbeat, can work, too. White noise made by machinery which is repetitive, such as the noise of a vacuum cleaner, hair dryer or washing machine is also said to have a soothing effect.

Sucking: some babies are sucky babies. They are not hungry but simply enjoy sucking and are comforted by it; it steadies their heart rate, relaxes them and generally helps them to settle. It doesn't seem to matter to them whether it's your nipple, your finger or a dummy. You will need to decide which you prefer. If you are happy for your baby to have a dummy – and that would free you up to do other things – sterilise it first before giving it to her. Most babies grow out of the sucking stage at around four months.

TOP TIP

While some babies hate being undressed and given a bath, others love it. The sound of the water running, and then the warmth of the bath and the feel of your hands touching her can all help to calm a crying baby.

Peace and quiet: at times your baby may be crying because she doesn't want to be fussed over any more, so being held will make her feel irritable. If this is the case then it's time to lie her down in her cot and leave her.

Baby massage

Rubbing and stroking your baby can have a wonderfully soothing effect, and skin-to-skin contact can help you and your baby bond. In recent years baby massage has become very popular as a way to reduce crying and encourage sleep.

First of all make sure that wherever you are going to massage your baby is warm and comfortable and that the atmosphere is quiet and calm. Try to choose a time of day when your baby isn't too tired or hungry, and don't massage her just after a feed because the rubbing movements may make her sick.

Lay your baby on her back on a soft towel and undress her. If you like you can rub olive oil into your hands, but in any event make sure that your hands are warm. If your baby doesn't seem to like it, then stop and try again another time. Most babies will love it, though.

Head:

1. With the flat of your hands, start at your baby's forehead and stroke both sides of her face down to her neck and back again.

2. Use a circular motion to lightly massage her forehead from the middle out to her ears.

3. Continue this circular motion behind her ears and around her head.

Chest and tummy:

1. Putting the flat of your hands on your baby's chest, gently massage her front using a circular motion from the middle up to her neck and then out to her sides.

2. Move your hands lower down to gently rub your baby's tummy.

Arms:

1. Use long strokes down her arms from top to bottom.

2. Take her hand and use your thumb in a circular motion to massage her palm. Then repeat the motion on her other palm.

TOP TIP
If your baby gets distressed when she is naked, simply massage her through her vest or sleepsuit instead.

Legs, feet and toes:

1. Stroke each leg gently with the whole of your hand, starting from the top of her thighs and working down. Bend her knees and push her leg up and then down again.

2. When you get to your baby's feet, start by pulling her toes gently and then rubbing the top of each foot with your thumb.

Turn your baby over carefully and use the same gentle circular movements to massage her back from her head to her bottom, and then down her legs to her feet.

By the time you have finished giving your baby a massage, both of you should feel more relaxed and calmed by the experience.

Crying in older babies: 3–12 months

Once your baby is three months old she will probably feel more settled and comfortable and should therefore cry less. On average a baby at this age cries for about an hour a day. As she gets older, her reasons for crying may change and may include:

Anxiety: as your baby becomes more aware of the world around her, she may become worried if her familiar world and routine changes. Strange and new situations may make her anxious if you're not with her. If this is the case, don't leave her with people she doesn't know or in a new environment.

Boredom: your older baby will need more of your attention to keep her stimulated. If you leave her alone, she will get bored and cry for your attention. Of course you cannot play with her all the time, but make sure she has things

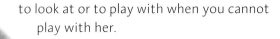
to look at or to play with when you cannot play with her.

Accidents: as your baby becomes mobile, she is more likely to hurt herself by knocking into things and bumping herself. Usually a hug, a kiss and a rub better are all that is needed to comfort her.

Teething: babies usually start teething at around five months, with a first tooth appearing from six months. While some babies don't seem to suffer any discomfort from teething, it does seem to cause crying in other babies. There are many different ointments or gels that can alleviate the discomfort. Chewing on a teething ring or another hard toy may also help.

How to cope with a crying baby

Living with a baby who cries a lot can be very difficult to cope with, especially if she cries a lot at night and stops you getting much sleep. You may have tried many techniques to soothe your baby but still she cries, or only stops for a short while before starting again. Here are some tips which may help to make coping a bit easier:

1. Remember that it isn't personal. Sometimes it can seem as though your baby is crying deliberately to wind you up, but it can help to remind yourself that small babies don't cry on purpose to upset you and they are not being naughty.

2. If it gets too much, put your baby in a cot or somewhere safe, shut the door and go to another room in the house for a few minutes. Try to take some deep breaths and calm yourself down before you go back to your baby.

3. Find support – talk to a friend or relative who might be able to help you. Your health visitor should be able to provide advice, too, and tell you about local support groups so that you can meet people in similar situations and share your experiences. Telephone helplines also exist, such as CRY-SIS *(see page 70)* which are open 24 hours a day to listen and offer advice and support.

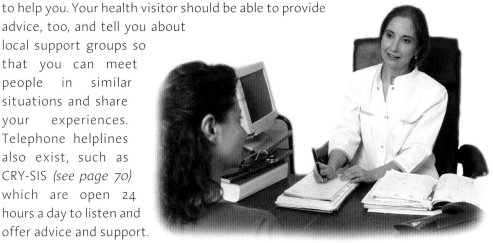

4. Ask someone to babysit for you now and again so that you get a bit of time off. Your partner or another family member can look after your baby for an hour or two while you go out and relax. Even leaving the house for half an hour can make you feel better.

TOP TIP

At times you might find your baby's crying frustrating but remember that however upset and anxious you become, you must *never* shake your baby to stop her crying.

Although it can be very difficult to live with a crying baby, it may help to know that the phase won't last long and that you and your baby will come through it and be fine. In the meantime, take comfort from the times when your baby smiles, and know that as she gets older she will cry less and smile more and more.

Chapter 6

PLAYING Why, what and how to play with your baby

Caring for your baby is not just about doing the practical things like feeding and dressing her. For her to develop and learn she needs your love, time and attention. By spending time with your baby and playing with her, you will be giving her all of these things while helping her to learn about the world she lives in.

As your baby develops and as her skills and abilities grow, the way you play with her will change – from quiet visual games when she is newborn to noisier active games by the end of her first year. Your baby will be able to develop her mental and physical skills through play and increase her confidence and sociability. Most importantly of all, she will develop a sense of fun. Playtime will be something that both you and your baby can enjoy.

Playing with your young baby

Playing with your baby is about stimulating her senses: sight, sound, smell and touch. She will enjoy hearing your voice, looking at your face, and being touched by you. By playing with your baby you will find out what toys and activities she does and doesn't like.

Talking and listening: you may have started talking to your baby even before she was born – she will certainly recognise your voice from hearing it when she was in the womb. Now that you can see her, talk to your baby as much as you can – while you are holding, feeding or changing her. It doesn't matter what you talk about as she won't know exactly what you're saying, but she will be able to understand that you are communicating with her. If you are patient and give her time, your baby will learn to respond by mimicking your sounds and facial expressions – in this way she will learn to talk back to you.

Reading: whatever her age, your child will enjoy and benefit from being read to, and the earlier you start the better. At 0–2 months your baby can see colours, but will have difficulty distinguishing between similar colours (such as red and orange). She will therefore respond better to contrasting colours, especially black and white. So you could start off by showing her cloth books in black and white with very simple patterns. After two months she will be able to distinguish between different shades and respond to any brightly coloured pictures. She will be able to see the shapes and be interested in them. From the beginning she will enjoy hearing your voice when you read to her, so a story at bedtime could become part of her routine. It doesn't have to be very long to begin with; gradually, your baby will start to understand the words and her vocabulary will increase as she listens.

From six months, your baby may enjoy sturdy boardbooks, which are almost impossible to destroy – although she can still chew them! Your baby will enjoy the repetition and the rhythm of nursery rhymes, and if you can sing the rhymes, even better!

Visual games: your young baby will not able to see far, but a mobile placed above her cot or her changing mat will fascinate her. She will be able to see the shapes moving as they bob around. Similarly, lying her on an activity mat with soft toys hanging down will keep her interested, especially if one of the toys has a reflective shine on one side. Babies love faces and although she won't realise it's her face she's looking at, she will be comforted by her reflection. Above all she will enjoy looking at your face, especially exaggerated facial expressions when you are holding her closely – wait to see if she tries to imitate you. You could also try sticking a picture of a face on her cot so she has something to look at when she wakes up.

From about six weeks you can prop your baby up in a bouncing chair so that she is better able to see her surroundings. She will enjoy just looking around but make sure she also has things near her, perhaps strapped to her chair, that she can look at and touch and keep herself entertained.

Once your baby is a few months old she will enjoy games like peek-a-boo, when you hide your face in your hands for a moment before revealing your face again and saying 'boo'. A variation is to cover her face with a muslin cloth or raggy toy and then remove it so she can see your smiling face again.

Touch and feel, physical and active games: games that involve movement can also be enjoyed from very early on. Holding your baby while you dance, sway and rock can be enjoyed by the youngest baby. After a few weeks she may enjoy being jiggled on your lap. After a few months she will probably enjoy games that involve bouncing her on your lap, starting off gently and bouncing her higher and higher. If you have an active baby, she may love being strapped into a baby bouncer so that she can bounce herself up and down.

TOP TIP
Remember, you should never leave your baby on her own in the bath, even for a moment, in case she slips.

She will also enjoy having her sense of touch stimulated. Try some of these games:

'Round and round the garden': take your baby's hand and uncurl her fingers with your hand. With your other hand, use a finger to move around the palm of her hand while you sing: 'Round and round the garden goes the teddy bear.' Then as you say 'One step, two steps,' walk your fingers up her arm and then tickle her under her arm as you say 'Tickle you under there.'

This Little Piggy: you may remember this toe game from your own childhood. Touch each toe, starting with the big toe, as you say: 'This little piggy went to market, this little piggy stayed at home. This little piggy had roast beef, this little piggy had none. And this little piggy cried "Wee, wee, wee!" all the way home', and tickle her again or give her a kiss.

Even if your baby didn't like bathtime initially, she may soon be able to enjoy very simple games with water, which will make bathtime fun:

Pouring water: if your baby is tiny, make sure that you are holding her securely with one hand, then with the other gently pour water onto her tummy. She will enjoy the sensation and the sound it makes. As she gets older, she will enjoy filling cups with water and pouring it out again, and she will learn from this activity, too.

Splashing: from around three months, your baby might enjoy the splashes she can make when she kicks her legs and waves her arms about. Before she notices

BATH TOYS
You don't have to buy special toys to put in the bath. Your baby will be happy with anything that floats, such as empty plastic bottles; anything that pours, such as plastic beakers; and anything that she can squeeze, such as a sponge.

she can do this herself, try taking her hand and patting it on the surface of the water.

How much to play with your baby

To begin with your new baby will probably not want to spend a lot of time playing, as most of her time will be spent either feeding or sleeping. Gradually, as she gets older, she will want to spend more time discovering the world and being stimulated through play. But there isn't a set amount of time you have to play with your baby – it depends on what you both enjoy doing. If you have a baby who sleeps a lot and is quite passive, you may play less with her than with a baby who is active, alert and demanding to be played with all the time. Your baby might take a keen interest in the world around her, but be quite able to take it in without needing your company and play happily for long periods of time on her own. Or your baby might hate being left alone and want you to be with her all the time.

Overstimulation: it's important to listen to your baby and to know when she's had enough. Watch her for signs that she's losing concentration or is getting tired. If you try to force her to play she will become irritable and upset. Try to stick with a game for a while rather than switching from one game to the next and bombarding her with lots of new experiences all at once. This will help her develop concentration skills, too.

Playing with your older, mobile baby

Once your baby is able to move around by herself your life will change quite dramatically! Everything within reaching distance is a potential toy for your baby and she will want to play with them all. She will explore, experiment and discover. She will also develop her physical coordination, as she moves herself around, pulling herself up to reach for things and satisfying her growing curiosity. It is likely she will become fascinated by ordinary household objects. Provided you

TOP TIP
Problem-solving games will encourage your baby to use her brain. If she doesn't manage to work them out straight away, be patient and give her some time. If she continues to have problems with a game, show her how to do it and then let her try again for herself.

have checked all objects for any potential risk to your baby, these can make great toys:

- Wooden spoons and pans – these make a great noise when banged together!

- Greaseproof paper – this can be scrunched up into a ball and makes an interesting noise.

- Boxes – great to put things into and take them out again.

- Anything that can be rolled – from empty cotton reels to tennis balls.

- Clear plastic bottles – fill these with small stones or dried pasta to make a good sound, or with coloured liquid to make them interesting to look at. Make sure the lid of the bottle is screwed on very tightly to avoid any of the contents spilling and causing a risk of your baby choking or drinking the coloured liquid.

From around nine months, your baby will have developed enough hand–eye coordination to enjoy the following:

- Stacking toys – plastic rings that fit on a post in varying sizes, nesting cups which your baby can work out how to fit inside each other, and wooden bricks to build towers out of and knock over again.

- Toys that make a noise if you press a button.

Be safe

Just before your baby is really mobile, you will need to check your house and garden for dangerous objects and childproof your home as far as possible. Here are some things to think about:

Cupboard locks: fix these to your cupboards to prevent your baby opening them with potential risk to herself as well as the things in your cupboard.

TOP TIP
If possible, leave one cupboard which she can open filled with plastic and unbreakable things she's allowed to play with.

Toxic products: items such as medicines and cleaning products must be kept well out of reach. From around five months, your baby will put everything she finds into her mouth.

Electric sockets: small fingers can easily fit into tiny holes. Make sure you have covers on electric sockets.

Plastic bags and balloons: a lot of bags do have holes in to prevent suffocation, but it's still better to keep them out of reach. A burst balloon can also smother a baby and cause suffocation or choking.

Strings, ribbons and cords: make sure these are out of reach so your baby can't wind them around herself. Also make sure there aren't any cords attached to heavy objects – such as an iron – which she could pull on top of her.

Table-top corners: look at your furniture and make sure that there is nothing that can hurt your baby. Low coffee tables with sharp corners are just the right height for your crawling baby to bump into.

Stairgates: make sure your baby can't go up or down stairs without you.

In the garden: if you have a pond or other water feature in your garden you will need to prevent your baby from getting to it. Look out for poisonous plants, and make sure that any garden tools are kept well out of reach.

When visiting other people's houses or your baby is in a new environment, you will need to keep an eye on her all the time to make sure she's safe.

Conclusion

Your baby's first year is one of enormous growth and development. She will change from being totally dependent on you for all her needs, to doing all sorts of things herself and probably not wanting you to help her (even though she may still need it!). You will have discovered who your baby is, what sort of character she has, and her likes and dislikes. Your baby may have learnt to walk already, or to say a few words, so you should be communicating easilywith each other. You will have both come a long way and achieved a huge amount: a wonderful beginning to a lifelong relationship that will continue to develop and grow.

USEFUL ORGANISATIONS

Association of Breastfeeding Mothers
ABM
PO Box 207
Bridgwater
Somerset
TA6 7YT
Counselling hotline: 08444 122 949
Website: www.abm.me.uk
Telephone advice service for breastfeeding mothers.

Cry-sis
BM Cry-sis
London
WC1N 3XX
Helpline: 08451 228 669
Website: www.cry-sis.org.uk;
A charity providing self-help and support to families with excessively crying, sleepless and demanding babies.

Foundation for the Study of Infant Deaths (FSID)
Artillery House
11-19 Artillery Row
London SW1P 1RT
Website: www.fsid.org.uk
Helpline: 020 7233 2090
Offers support and education to parents and professionals on reducing the risk of Sudden Infant Death Syndrome (SIDS).

La Leche League (Great Britain)
PO Box 29
West Bridgford
Nottingham
NG2 7NP
Phone: 0845 456 1855 (Mondays and Thursdays, answerphone at other times)
Website: www.laleche.org.uk
Personal counselling and local groups to give help and information to women who want to breastfeed.

National Childbirth Trust (NCT)
Alexandra House
Oldham Terrace
Acton
London
W3 6NH
General enquiry line: 0870 770 3236
Breastfeeding line: 0870 444 8708 (9am to 6pm, seven days a week)
Website: www.nct.org.uk
Ante- and postnatal classes giving information and help to mothers.

Tamba
2 The Willows
Gardner Road
Guildford
GU1 4PG
Phone: 0870 770 3305
Website: www.tamba.org.uk
Provides information and mutual support networks for families of twins, triplets and more.

INDEX

INDEX

1 3 5 7 9 10 8 6 4 2

Published in 2008 by Vermilion, an imprint of Ebury Publishing

A Random House Group Company

Copyright © Naia Edwards 2008

All photographs © Photolibrary Group

Naia Edwards has asserted her right to be identified as the author of this Work in accordance with the Copyright, Designs and Patents Act 1988

The Random House Group Limited Reg. No. 954009

Addresses for companies within the Random House Group can be found at www.randomhouse.co.uk

A CIP catalogue record for this book is available from the British Library

The Random House Group Limited makes every effort to ensure that the papers used in our books are made from trees that have been legally sourced from well-managed and credibly certified forests. Our paper procurement policy can be found on www.rbooks.co.uk/environment

To buy books by your favourite authors and register for offers visit www.rbooks.co.uk

Printed and bound in Singapore by Tien Wah Press

ISBN 9780091923426

Please note that conversions to imperial weights and measures are suitable equivalents and not exact.

The information given in this book should not be treated as a substitute for qualified medical advice; always consult a medical practitioner. Neither the author nor the publisher can be held responsible for any loss or claim arising out of the use, or misuse, of the suggestions made or the failure to take medical advice.